NUGGETS
to Live By

LINDA FAYE ANDERSON

ISBN 978-1-64492-593-5 (paperback)
ISBN 978-1-64492-594-2 (digital)

Copyright © 2019 by Linda Faye Anderson

All rights reserved. No part of this publication may be reproduced, distributed, or transmitted in any form or by any means, including photocopying, recording, or other electronic or mechanical methods without the prior written permission of the publisher. For permission requests, solicit the publisher via the address below.

Christian Faith Publishing, Inc.
832 Park Avenue
Meadville, PA 16335
www.christianfaithpublishing.com

Unless marked otherwise, the scripture references in this book were taken from the New International Version (NIV) of the Bible. Quotes used from other versions were marked accordingly such as the New King James Version (NKJV), and the New Living Translation (NLT) of the Bible.

Printed in the United States of America

To my son, David Anderson II; my daughter, Phylicia Renee Hills; and to all Christians (new and old) who are learning how to live this Christian life.

Contents

Acknowledgments 7
Introduction 9
Chapter 1   The Greatest Love Story Ever Told 11
Chapter 2   We Need the Blood 16
Chapter 3   How to Lead a Sinner to Christ 18
Chapter 4   Intimacy with God 21
Chapter 5   Waiting on God 25
Chapter 6   Forgiveness 36
Chapter 7   Sin and the Gray Areas 41
Chapter 8   Your Gifts and Talents Are Needed 46
Chapter 9   Love Your Neighbor as You Love Yourself ...49
Chapter 10 Spiritual Warfare 54
Chapter 11 Judgement Day Is Coming 63

Acknowledgments

First and foremost, I want to acknowledge God for blessing me with this assignment and for anointing me to write this book.

I would also like to acknowledge my awesome husband, David Anderson, for encouraging me as I embarked upon writing this book and for the time he spent proofreading this book.

Thank you sweetie! I could not have completed this book without you.

Introduction

On August 19, 2018, I was awakened from a dream at 5:30 a.m. In the dream, a very important executive sent a message saying she wanted to see me. I knew our meeting would be very important. In the dream, I went into my shoe closet and began to look for the right shoes to wear. I was having a hard time finding the right pair of shoes. I didn't want to keep her waiting, but I wanted to have on the perfect pair of shoes for the meeting. When I finally found the shoes I thought were perfect, I headed over to the office where we were going to meet, and to my horror, she was leaving and stated that she could no longer wait. I woke up from that dream baffled. For you see, I had been waiting on God to give me instructions on what He wanted me to write about. I asked the Lord what the dream meant, because the obvious interpretation seemed to be that I had missed my opportunity, because I took too long.

The Lord told me that the dream was a warning to me. He impressed upon me that when He gives me instructions (about writing this book), I should not wait until I think everything is perfect to start writing. He caused me to understand that now is the time for me to write this book.

This book is not being written for Bible scholars. This book is being written for new Christians and those who are trying to figure out what this Christian journey is all about. Those of us who have been walking with the Lord for years need to reach back and help the new converts by sharing our experiences and our knowledge with them. I pray that the things I have learned over the past forty-five years of walking with the Lord will help someone in their journey.

CHAPTER 1

The Greatest Love Story Ever Told

Let's begin by discussing how much God loves us.

In St. John 3:16, it tells us, "For God so loved the world that He gave His only begotten Son, that whoever believes in Him should not perish but have everlasting life" (NKJV). God had a master plan from the beginning when he created us in His image. God wanted a bride as seen in Isaiah 62:5. Also in Revelation 21:9, God referred to us as His bride, the wife of the Lamb. Genesis 24 tells us the story of how Abraham sent his servant to find a bride for his son Isaac. That account is a type and shadow of God sending His Holy Spirit to seek out a bride for His son, Jesus. We are that bride!

There are many more references to God calling us His bride, but we will look at one more. In Matthew 25, starting at verse one, Jesus gave a parable of five wise and five foolish virgins (the virgins represented Christians) who were waiting for the bridegroom (Jesus) to return. When you read this passage, you find that the five wise virgins made all the proper preparations to meet the bridegroom. However, the five foolish virgins were not ready. They did not prepare, and they ran out of the oil they needed to keep their lamps burning. (In the old days, lamps were used that operated with oil in the bottom and a cotton wick long enough to reach the oil that would keep the lamp burning when the wick was lit. Google oil wick or oil lamp to get a picture of what I am referring to.) When the five that ran out of oil left to get more oil, the bridegroom came and the five that were ready (who had plenty of oil in their lamps) went to meet the bridegroom, and the door was shut. When the five unprepared virgins came back with the oil, it was too late. They were not allowed to get in.

The moral of the parable is that we as Christians need to allow God to prepare us for his return. *All we must do is be obedient and follow the leading of the spirit—go where He tells us to go and do what He tells us to do and we will be ready when He returns.* I believe those that missed out are those Christians that are not taking their new birth seriously and who feel they have all the time in the world to do whatever *they* want to do.

The Bible tells us, no man knows the day or hour of Jesus's return. We need to live each day as though this is the day of His return. When we mess up, ask for forgiveness and get it right quickly. Don't take advantage of this time of grace that we are in. Just because God's judgement has not fallen on you for the sins you are engaging in right now does not mean it's ok to keep practicing that sin. Repent (turn from that thing and stop it) while we are still in the time of God's grace. We want to be ready when Jesus comes back which could be at any time.

I believe that once we understand who we are to God, we can see and understand the purpose in all that we are going through. Everything is working together for our good as it tells us in Romans 8:28. To understand who we are, we need to start from the beginning.

Adam and Eve—Paradise Lost

Let's go back to the garden. Adam and Eve had it made. They were living in paradise, walking and talking with God. They had one commandment to follow. God told them *not* to eat from the tree of the knowledge of good and evil.

There has been a lot of conversations about why God gave us a free will. It is simple. God did not want us to be robots. He wanted us to be His by choice. He wanted us to obey Him, because we love Him. Well we know the story: Eve listened to the serpent and disobeyed God, and they were subsequently kicked out of the garden. Paradise lost! (Genesis 3:24)

Jesus Christ—Restoration

Do you think for one minute that their actions were a surprise to God? Remember, God is all knowing. He knew Adam and Eve were going to make the wrong choice. He already had a plan for our redemption. *God loved us so much that He came down to earth in the person of Jesus Christ to redeem us back to Him.* Romans 5:15-19 tells us that by one man's obedience (Jesus), we received the gift of righteousness. Romans 5:8 tells us that while we were yet sinners, Christ died for us.

Yes! Jesus loves us! He that knew no sin, became sin for us. He took our place on the cross. Blood had to be shed for our sins to be forgiven. God had to honor his own law that stated, "without the shedding of blood there is no forgiveness of sin" (Hebrews 9:22). We owe our lives to Jesus. God loved us so much that *He came after us*!

Holy Spirit

God, in all His knowledge, knew that we would need all the help we could get to make it back to Him. So not only did He come down to earth to redeem us in the person of Jesus Christ, He sent the Holy Spirit to live in us to be our counselor, teacher, and to lead us into all truth (John 16:13).

Keep in mind, we are on a journey back to our Father. The blood of Jesus makes us righteous. Although we are righteous in the eyes of God, we still have flaws and make mistakes. God sees the end as if it has already happened. However, in our daily experiences, we are going through the process of being saved. It goes along with the statement that seems confusing (but it is not) that says, *we have been saved, we are being saved, and we shall yet be saved.* The carnal mind cannot understand that statement. But it makes perfect sense. When

Jesus died on the cross He said, "It is finished." The work was done. Jesus, by one sacrifice, forever paid the price (*we have been saved*). Through our trials and tests and daily experiences, *we are being saved*. Philippians 2:12 tells us to work out our salvation with fear and trembling. This means there is something we must do. Finally, when Christ returns, we will be changed in a moment in a twinkling of an eye (1 Corinthians 15:52). *We shall be saved*!

Trials and Tests

This is where we are right now. We are being molded and made via the trials and the tests that God allows to come our way. We really don't like it much. Nobody wants to go through struggles, but to be perfected, we must go through the fire. God told me once that anything that goes through the fire comes out changed. Have you been in the fire lately? If there was another way for the job to get done, God would have allowed it. But there is no other way. I have learned that our human nature will not budge unless there is a fire put under us. Hebrews 12:11 tells us that no chastening for the moment is joyous, *but afterward, it will produce righteousness* in us.

In James 1:2–4, we are reminded to count it all joy when we are being tested because it is producing patience in us. In Acts 5:41, the apostles did just that. After they were persecuted, they left rejoicing that they were counted worthy to suffer for Christ. James 1:12 tells us that all those who go through the testing will receive a crown of life promised to all those who love Him.

Aren't you glad that trouble doesn't last always. There is an expiration date for your troubles. All that Job (recorded in the Old Testament) went through: he lost his property and all his children, boils on his body, etc.; his trials had an expiration date. He received double for his trouble. (Job 42:10) That should encourage us to hold on a little longer. Our blessing is right around the corner.

We must remember that the trials and tests are part of the process God is using to make us that church that is without spot or wrinkle. The trials we are going through now will ensure we are ready when Jesus comes back for us. He is cleansing His bride. God loves us too much to let us stay the way we are.

Christ Will Return

Take heart fellow Christian, our King is coming back for His bride, and His rewards will be with him. We need to encourage one another with the anticipation of His return. In Genesis 24, when Abraham's servant found the bride for Isaac (Rebecca) and was taking her back to meet him for the first time, I'm sure she encouraged herself by looking at all the jewelry and earrings He had brought for her. After all, she was on her way to marry a man she had never met. We also need to look at the gifts our heavenly father has given us when we get discouraged and encourage ourselves to keep on walking to meet Him. Revelation 21:1–7 tells us that when we get to heaven, there will be no more tears, pain, or sorrow. What a day that shall be!

We are recipients of *the greatest love story ever told*. Every day is a new adventure as we travel on our journey. Be encouraged, our bridegroom is working things out on our behalf, and He is coming back for us.

> Nuggets: *God loves you so much that He left heaven and came down to this earth to save you.*
>
> Also remember: *Anything that goes through the fire comes out changed.*

Chapter 2

We Need the Blood

In Hebrews 9:22, it tells us that the law requires blood to remit (or forgive) our sins. The Old Testament records all the sacrifices that had to be made by God's people to atone (pay for) their sins. Every year these same sacrifices had to be made (they killed bulls, goats, sheep, and birds) for their sins to be forgiven. What a task! But if you wanted God to forgive you, that is what you had to do constantly. The Bible says in Hebrews 10:14 that Jesus, by *one sacrifice (himself), paid the price to take away our sins forever*! Let's just have a *selah* moment (pause and think about that).

Do we really understand what Jesus did for us? No more killing bulls and goats to have our sins covered for just one year. His death covers our sins: past, present, and future. Jesus does not have to come back and die again if we make another mistake or fall into sin. We need only to look to the cross and ask Him to forgive us. Don't take advantage of this time of grace that we are living in. The Bible says, if we sin, Jesus will be our advocate (He will always go to God on our behalf and fight for us by way of His shed blood). He has already paid the price for our forgiveness.

When Jesus died, Matthew 27:51 tells us, the veil (curtain) in the temple was torn from top to bottom, the earth shook, the rocks split, and many deceased saints were raised from their graves and were seen by many people! Wow! Jesus was on a mission when He came here. The plan was always to come here to die and redeem us after Adam and Eve made a mess of things. Jesus accomplished His mission. While we were yet sinners, Christ died for us (Romans 5:8)!

Thank God for Jesus! Had he not died for us, we would all still be condemned and on our way to hell. Jesus (who is God in the flesh) came and got us! Does He love us or what? We needed grace; we needed mercy, so God covered us with his blood which is his grace and mercy. Imagine that you are naked. Picture the blood of Jesus as a giant red blanket that God just wrapped around you so that you are no longer exposed and naked. His blood justified us. Someone explained the word justified to mean—*just as if I never sinned*. Our sins have all been washed away because of what Jesus did. He is awesome! We can never thank Him enough.

When it talks about the veil of the temple ripping all by itself, what that means is that when Jesus died, He opened the way for us to meet and talk directly to God. There is nothing separating us from our God now. We don't have to go to a priest to tell him about our sins. When we fall short, we can go directly to Father God and say, "God forgive me." Another awesome thing about Jesus is that He will always be praying for us and has saved us completely (Hebrews 7:25).

The final thing I will say about the blood of Jesus is that His blood is the only way to the Father. He said, "I am the way, the truth, and the life and *no one comes to the Father except through me*" (John 14:6). Read it for yourself, because there are a lot of false teachings out there saying that Jesus is not the only way to get to heaven. If you believe the word of God, *Jesus is the only way to get to the Father!*

> Nugget: How important is the blood? Again, think of yourself as being naked and the blood of Jesus as a giant red blanket that has been wrapped around you to cover your nakedness. This same blood also takes away all your sins, and God remembers them no more (Psalms 103:12, Hebrews 8:12).

CHAPTER 3

How to Lead a Sinner to Christ

Now since we know how important the blood is and the truth that Jesus is the only way to the Father, we need to make sure we lead as many people as we can to Christ. The great commission is as follows (Matthew 28:19-20):

> Therefore, go and make disciples of all nations, baptizing them in the name of the Father and of the Son and of the Holy Spirit, and teaching them to obey everything I have commanded you. And surely, I am with you always, to the very end of the age.

Do you realize this great commission (the above noted passage) is not just for ministers and pastors? All Christians should know how to win a soul for Christ. But before we go there, we need to make sure we are being a good witness for Christ and not bringing shame to His name. Some people are closet Christians, because they are afraid if people know they are trying to live right, they will be judged by all their faults. Let me put your mind at ease, *God knows we are not perfect!* He chooses us anyway just as we are.

If you are presently doing what God has told you to do and living the way God has directed you to live, you are walking perfectly before Him. Read the Bible. God used a lot of imperfect people. David took another man's wife and had him killed. Moses was wanted for murder. Jacob was so slick he stole his brother's birthright and blessing. Peter denied Jesus and lied saying he did not know him. Paul, before he was slain in the spirit, went around persecuting God's people (he ended up writing most of the New Testament). Jonah did not obey God until he was swallowed by a big fish. If God could use all those messed up people, He can use you and me just as we are.

Do people look at you and wonder what is so different about you? Do they think secretly, *I want what they have*? Or are you trying so hard not to be different that you have succeeded, and people can't see any difference between you and your lifestyle and theirs? Why would they see a need to come to Christ if we look and act just like them: cursing, fighting, no self-control, losing our temper, talking about people behind their backs, not doing our job at work or half doing our job, turning up (I believe that is the term used) more than the sinner?

In Matthew 5:16, it tells us to let your light so shine before men that they may see your good works and glorify your Father which is in heaven. As Christians, we are representing God here on this earth. The last thing we should want to do is shame His name. I am not talking about us being robots or acting like we are perfect. I'm talking about realizing that you belong to Jesus, and your life should show some resemblance of Him.

Think about how our children resemble us, and people can look at them and say, "Yep, that's your child. He [or she] looks just like you." Well Father God is desiring the same thing: for people to look at us and think, there is something different about them. He/she must be a Christian or a woman or man of God.

I'm not your judge; search yourself: are you allowing the flesh to be in the forefront, and that is what everyone sees, or are you letting the spirit man in you take the lead? If we want to win a soul to Christ, make sure we are not a hindrance but a positive testimony for Jesus. Okay, let's move on.

A lot of people feel they don't need Jesus. They look at themselves as not being a bad person, so they think they are okay. We must get them to recognize that they need a savior. You can start by asking them some questions. A question I like to ask is, "Have you given any thought to where you want to spend eternity?" I also let them know, "You only have two choices. You will either spend eternity with God or in hell." At this point, I would recite to them Romans 10:9, "If you declare *with your mouth*, 'Jesus is Lord,' and believe in *your* heart that God raised him from the dead, you will be saved."

At this point I would ask them to accept Christ today by repeating the following prayer (have them repeat it after you).

1. Lord, I believe You died for my sins.
2. I repent and ask You to forgive me for my sins.
3. I ask You to come into my heart and be my Lord and savior.

Finally I would say, with that simple prayer, I welcome you to the family of God. Start a prayer life (begin talking to God as if He was your best friend), start reading the Bible (on line if you don't have one), and find a church that teaches the Bible, so you can begin to grow in the Lord. God bless you!

If it is someone you know, give them your contact information in case they have any questions later. There are many ways to lead a person to Christ. Some are more complicated. Try not to be too wordy when the person is repeating after you to avoid confusing them. I find it is better to keep it simple. The above is just an example that you are free to use.

> Nugget: Luke 15:7 tells us that heaven rejoices more over one soul that is saved than it does over ninety-nine righteous people who don't need to be saved. Let God use you in winning souls for Christ. It is part of our responsibility (great commission). You can do it!

Chapter 4

Intimacy with God

Once we are saved, we need to work on becoming more intimate with God. Spending time in God's presence should be first on our priority list. When you first wake-up in the morning, before your feet hit the floor and before you think about anything else, put your mind on the Lord. Tell Him how much you love and adore Him. Tell Him how you cannot imagine your life without Him. Listen in case He wants to speak something into your spirit. For example, sometimes He wakes me up with a song that I have not heard in years or with a scripture that encourages my heart. As you lie there, remember how good He has been to you. Begin thanking Him for your bed, your home, your family, your job, your finances, etc. Thank Him for whatever situation you are in, even if you do not understand it (because you know God is working it out for your good).

If you are in a situation that is very difficult for you to handle, remember, this is our time with the Lord, so talk to Him. Tell Him how you really feel. For example, "God I am really having a hard time with _____ (insert the name of whoever you are struggling with), please help me in this situation."

My conversations with my Daddy (I sometimes refer to God as my Daddy) are not always nice and sweet. I have had to literally say, "God I don't think I can take this anymore. I need You to work this situation out for me." Guess what, when we ask for His help, He will help us.

To have an intimate relationship with God, we must remain in a state of readiness, always staying in tune with Him. Stay on the right channel! What do I mean by that? Feed your spirit man by reading the Bible daily if possible. The book of Psalms is a good place to start. As Christians, we need to know the word. We need to study to show ourselves approved, so we can rightly divide the word of truth (2 Timothy 2:15). There is really no excuse for us not to be learning the word. If we don't have time to just sit down and read it, order the CDs called the *Bible Experience*. I used those CDs to teach my son the Bible. We would have about a half hour ride to get to school every morning, so I would put in the CD and away we went—on our way to drop him off at school and being filled with the word.

Another way to stay in tune with God is to listen to spiritual songs. It is hard for the enemy to get your attention if you are reading your word or singing uplifting songs. Before I retired from my job, whenever I felt stressed at work, I would go into my office, lock my door, and take a five-minute praise break to just sing and dance around my office until the heaviness lifted. The Lord and I had some good times in that office. If you don't have an office, you can take a bathroom break, or take a walk outside on your break to clear your head. If you are unable to leave your workstation, just have a praise service right where you are (but don't stop working).

I am all for balance. Don't go to work and tell your boss you need time to take a praise break when they are depending on you to do a job. God is wise, and He teaches us to do things decently and in order. You are there to do a job; make sure you do it well (that's a testimony to God). God will open doors for you to get breaks. If you can have a radio, keep your radio on a station that will feed your spirit. Music came from God and is powerful. Remember in the Bible when David would play music for Saul when he was being tormented by evil spirits (1 Samuel 16:23). I like a variety of music, but when I am in a spiritual battle, I'll play Hillsong or something that will edify my spirit.

Occasionally spend time before the Lord in silence, just lying in his presence. We should not always have a *grocery list* of things we want God to do for us. Think about a natural relationship. Think about how happy it makes a man if his woman is not with him just for what he can do for her, but she's with him, because she loves spending time with him. God is the same way. He loves it when we come before Him just to sit in his presence and just to love on Him and let His love flow over us. It is so awesome to sit in His presence. Make sure you have those times with Him. It is during these times of intimacy that we can hear God speaking to us in that still small voice. Some of you are thinking, "Well, God never talks to me." I can almost guarantee that God has been talking to you, but you have not recognized His voice. Have you ever been awakened with a praise song ringing in your head, or has God ever brought someone to your mind, and you immediately knew that you needed to pray for that person? If you did not pray for them, from this day forward, when someone's face flashes before you or you are thinking about someone strongly, *pray* for them right at that moment. We are connected as Christians even if we are on the other side of town. We have the same royal blood flowing through our veins. Therefore, it is not unusual to feel someone's pain who lives on the other side of town or even in another country. We are one body!

Have you ever had a strong tug not to drive down a certain street or take a certain expressway or go to a certain function? That was God leading and guiding you. The scriptures that come to your mind, that's God speaking to you and trying to tell you something. We should also learn to recognize God's voice when he speaks through others: pastors, ministers, friends, children, etc. God will get our attention anyway He can. God said in John 10:27–28, "My sheep hear My voice, and I know them, and they follow Me. And I give them eternal life, and they shall never perish; neither shall anyone snatch them out of My hand." According to this verse, we will be able to recognize His voice no matter where it is coming from or who or what he uses to speak to us.

As we grow in God, we begin to see Him and hear Him in places that we might not expect. I have recognized God speaking to me through a movie. For example, in the very first *Matrix* movie, when Neo finally start believing that he was *the one*, and he stood there effortlessly fighting the enemy with one hand. Watching that scene, I was reminded that when we truly know who we are, life will be effortless for us as well. A lot of our stress and worry comes because we are still not convinced that we are the King's kids. We belong to Jesus, and we are invincible.

Journaling is another way to become more intimate with God. In journaling, you keep a pad and pen available, and you write down your thoughts.

Those of us who are married know that you must make time to be intimate with your spouse. Well it is the same with God. We must make time to spend with Him. Another way to say this is for us to make sure we stay *plugged* into the source (God); otherwise, our battery will run down, and our light will get dim. When you notice that you are unusually short with people and everything irritates you, it is usually a sign that your *battery is getting low*. In other words, you need to spend some time with God (who is your source) and feed your spirit.

> Nugget: Remember that old song, "Oh what peace we often forfeit, oh what needless pains we bare, all because we do not carry everything to God in prayer." We find our peace when we are in His presence.

CHAPTER 5

Waiting on God

Waiting on God is something we are learning to do. The truth of the matter is *we don't like to wait*! I think it is in our nature (the old nature, that is) to be impatient. We want what we want when we want it. Oftentimes, if we don't get what we want when we want it, we tend to throw temper tantrums. When a child doesn't get his or her way, they throw a tantrum: kicking, screaming and yelling, having a pity party, and blaming everybody else. Oh, you don't think we throw tantrums?

Kicking

When we are kicking, we are saying, "God, if You don't do this for me, I'll have to do it for myself, because I am tired of waiting and going through this. I am going to make something happen with or without You, God, because You are taking entirely too long for me." Okay, we might not say those exact words to God, but our actions say it loud and clear. How many times have we messed things up because we put our hands to it? That did not work out for Abraham and Sarah, and it will not work out for us either.

We know the story. God promised Abraham and Sarah a child in Genesis 12:1–2. God told Abraham to leave his people and country and that He would make him into a great nation. In verse seven of that same chapter, God said, "To your offspring I will give this land" (Canaan). Abraham was seventy-five years old at that time. In Genesis 18, God sent messengers to Abraham and said, "I will surely return to you about this time next year and Sarah your wife will have a son." Abraham was well in his nineties now. In the fullness of time in Genesis 21:2, Isaac was born, and the promise was fulfilled (Abraham was now one hundred years old. We are talking about *twenty-five years of waiting*).

I am so glad that God put the whole story in the Bible! Abraham and Sarah did not patiently *wait*. Ten years after God gave them the promise (before Isaac was born), Sarah decided that ten years was long enough to wait, and God was taking too long, so she had to do something to *make it happen*. As a result, in Genesis 16:3, she told Abraham to sleep with Hagar, her servant, and that would be the way they would have children. Dear reader, what are you trying to make happen in your life because you are tired of waiting on God? We should always pray over everything, and don't make a move until God says *go*.

Women, we must be very careful in the area of *making it happen*. Most women know how to *get it done*. My husband told me once that God doesn't always tell me what He's up to (I'm paraphrasing), because I will try to help God out. Although I did not like hearing him say that, I knew he was right. Often, I picture myself at a starting line anxious to start a race, and I'm just waiting for the whistle to be blown. Truthfully, I believe it is in our nature as women to *get it done*.

Thank God for my husband who balances me out. There have been times when I jumped out there ready to go, and my husband would be the voice of reason to pull my coattail, and say, "Honey, let's wait or pray about it." There have also been times when he just flat out said, "No! I don't feel we should do that."

One example of that was some years ago. We were in Florida, at a resort, and they were trying to get us to buy into a time-share. I had looked at the film and saw all the pictures, and I was so ready to sign on the dotted line. I looked at my husband, and he said, "No, I'm not feeling that." I was so mad at him; I felt like someone had just poured cold water on me. Thank God I had sense enough, even way back then, to know that you don't make any major purchases like that until you are both in agreement. When we got home from Florida, we had an unexpected financial crisis, and had we bought the time-share, we would have been in financial trouble.

Lesson learned: stay under your covering women even if you don't like it. For those that aren't married, God uses your pastor, the Holy Spirit, a family member, and even a close friend to provide you with the checks and balances you need in life. Trust me, God will make sure you get the message by any means necessary.

One last thing about kicking. In Acts 9:5 (King James Version of the Bible), God told Paul, "…it is hard for you to kick against the pricks." A prick was a stick that farmers used in the Old Testament while plowing in their fields. This stick had a sharp piece of iron on its tip that would be used to steer the ox in the right direction. At times, the animal would rebel and kick at the prick; however, this would only bring the animal more pain. The more an ox kicked and rebelled, the prick would be pushed deeper into its flesh causing more pain. The more it rebelled, the more it suffered.

Are you getting a revelation about now? Wow! We need to stop fighting against the path God has for us. The more we fight against God, the more painful situations we will have to go through. God is going to get us where He wants us to be, but we can surely cause our way to be hard when it does not have to be. Sometimes, we are the hold up, not God.

When God led the children of Israel out of Egypt (you know the story in Exodus after they had been in bondage for over 400 years). Moses could have taken them to the promised land in *eleven days* (it was an eleven-day journey), but it took them *forty years* mainly because of their unbelief (see Numbers 14:11). Stop kicking! You really don't want to be stuck in the place you are in for the next forty years because you are in rebellion or too afraid to move. Just say what Jesus said, "Not my will, but thine be done."

Say this simple prayer: "Lord whatever You want me to do, I'll do. Wherever You want me to go, I'll go. I surrender this day to You." Amen!

Screaming and Yelling

Back to the tantrums we throw while waiting: screaming and yelling. When that child screams and yells because he or she is not getting his or her way, they do it to get attention. How many times have we said in our lifetime, "God, where are You? Are you even listening to me?"

You pray, and you feel like your prayers are not even leaving the ground. Don't you hate it when God is silent? When we get finished pouring our heart out, telling God why He needs to move and do something now, we still must wait! Or how many times have we said, "God, I'm done. I can't take it anymore." *Silence*!

I don't pretend to have figured God out, because Romans 11:34 reads, "Who has known the mind of the Lord? Or who has been his counselor?" There is another scripture that tells us that our thoughts are not His thoughts, and our ways are not His ways (Isaiah 55:8). God has a plan for us, and He has promised that He would not put more on us than we can bear. In Deuteronomy 8:2, it tells us that God led the children of Israel in the wilderness for forty years to humble them and reveal what was in their hearts.

Our trials and tests are not only to burn out the dross (faults); the trials also show us the power of God that is in us to overcome every test. Some of us have gone through some very tough situations, and as we look back over our life, many of us wonder how we made it through our trials, but we did, and we are still standing.

We tend to forget that the same power that raised Jesus from the dead lives in us! We have the almighty God living inside us; we cannot be defeated. We are more than conquerors. We are victorious. The next time you feel like screaming and yelling because you are tired of waiting, remember the scripture in Psalm 27:14, "Wait for the LORD; be strong and take heart and wait for the LORD."

Instead of screaming and yelling, just pray, "Father, I don't understand why I must go through this, but I love You with all my heart, and I know that You said You would never leave me or forsake me. So even though I can't see You in this situation right now, and even though I don't feel Your presence right now, I know that

You are with me, and I will trust You to bring me through this." Amen!

Self-Pity

Have you ever had a pity party when you did not get what you wanted? Although we might not want to admit it, most of us have had a pity party at one time or another. Have you ever said or thought the following? "Lord, I'm living right all I know how, and nothing seems to go right for me. My enemies seem to be doing better than I am." Psalm 37:9 reads that the wicked will eventually be destroyed. Stop worrying about your enemy. God will take care of our enemies, and remember, He said, "Vengeance is mine. I will repay."

Another problem we have as Christians is comparing ourselves to others. Dear reader, stop comparing yourself to other Christians. It might be their season for prosperity and the overflow of blessings. You might be in a cold season of testing. Take heart, your prosperity season will come as well. We must remember that our times are in His hands and that we all must go through seasons. Have you ever said, "Lord, what about me? I am happy for them, but what about me?"

Dear reader, you must know that *God is still in control, and He has not nor will He ever forget about you!* He said He loves you with an everlasting love. He knows the number of hairs on your head. You know what else He says about you? *You are the apple of His eye. No good thing will He withhold from you. We are the objects of His affection.* How cool is that!

I love living in Michigan, because I love the fact that we see all four seasons: winter, spring, summer, fall. Think about the four seasons for a moment; we have no say so in whether we will have a mild winter or a very cold winter or a very hot summer vs. a cool summer. But what we do know is when the season comes, we will go through it. If it gets below zero, we will just put more layers on to stay warm. If it gets too hot in the summer, we will wear less clothes, etc. The point is we adjust and get through it. Well it is the same with our spiritual seasons. If this is your season to be still and wait, guess what, you will learn to be still and wait. Remember, you are on the potter's wheel, and He knows exactly what kind of molding is needed to get the vessel He desires. So whatever season you find yourself in today, trust God. He knows what He is doing even if you don't. He meant what He said about never leaving you or forsaking you. Romans 8:28 reminds us that all things are working together for our good. Do we really believe what that scripture says? If we really believed that scripture, we would not stress and feel sorry for ourselves, because we would know that no matter what it looks like now, God is going to turn this situation around to work out for our good.

The Blame Game

We have been dealing with this blame game since the fall in the garden. Adam blamed Eve. Eve blamed the snake. Have you noticed that you tend to get irritable when you are waiting on God, and He doesn't answer when you think He should? As women, we can make life miserable for everyone in the house when we are not content or at peace. We should not be the cause of discord in our homes. That goes for men as well. When you are not at peace, you can affect your entire household. I have found that it helps when I feel myself getting frustrated to put on praise music (I love Hillsong; they seem to really know how to take you there), or a word tape. If it is service time, make sure you go to service to refresh yourself.

There are also some natural things we can do to relieve the stress and frustration of waiting. Go for a brisk walk, or take a long soak bath with candles and music. Some years back, before I retired from my job, I became really stressed at work (normal office politics). I remember coming home and renting all *Madea*'s plays (written by Tyler Perry) that were out at that time, and I would put them on just so that I could laugh about something. It worked. We should avoid making life miserable for everyone in our household just because we are frustrated and tired of waiting for God to move. What you are going through is nobody's fault. God has allowed you to be in this situation to get your attention. Instead of seeking to blame someone, ask God what He wants you to learn while waiting. We should look at everything God takes us through as a learning situation, and try to find the nugget. From this day forward, in every situation you go through, ask God, "What is the nugget in this situation?" We want to learn our lessons well, because some situations are so painful, we definitely do not want to *go around that mountain again*! Just know that if you do not learn the lesson God has for you in your present situation, you will go around the mountain again! If you find yourself blaming everybody for your problems, that is a good indication that you have not found the nugget yet (learned what you are supposed to learn), and you might as well get ready to go around the mountain again. He might use different people, or the situation might be a little different, but if God has a lesson for you to learn, He will make sure you get it before moving you to the next level in your spiritual walk.

Don't Put God on Your Time Frame

We must recognize that God is not limited by time. God does not look at time the way we do. Remember it reads in 2 Peter 3:8 that with the Lord a day is like a thousand years and a thousand years is like one day. Learn how to say, "Lord, however long it takes, I will be right here waiting for You to speak to me, move in me, or change the situation."

For a people who will live forever, we sure get bogged down with time. When God gives us a glimpse of the ministry He has called us to, we want it to start or happen *now*. After all, we feel that we are ready to launch that ministry now. *Waiting is a part of your preparation and training*! The Bible has numerous examples of people that had to wait for God to move. Here are a few examples:

> *Abraham*: We have already discussed how Abraham and Sarah had to wait for *twenty-five years* before they received the promised son (Genesis 21).

Joseph: After having dreams of what God had called him to, Joseph waited *thirteen years* from the time his brothers sold him into slavery to the time God's promise was fulfilled, and He became second in command in Egypt (Genesis 37).

Moses: After killing an Egyptian (to protect his fellow Israelite) and then fleeing to Midian, Moses waited *forty years* before God sent him back to deliver all his people (Exodus 3).

David: David had to wait *twenty-two years* from the time he was first anointed as king until he actually became King over *all* of Israel (2 Samuel 5).

Jesus: After being found in the temple with the teachers in Jerusalem at age twelve, Jesus went back and submitted to Joseph and Mary until he became thirty years old (waited a total of *eighteen years*) (Luke 2:41–52).

Think about Jesus, our elder brother, the first fruits among many brethren. He is the pattern son, the alpha and omega, the first and the last, the beginning and the end (Revelation 22:13). He is the great *I am*, the king of kings, and the lord of lords. There is none greater than Him. There are not enough adjectives to describe our precious Lord! But consider the fact that after waiting for eighteen years, knowing what He was called to do, it only took Him approximately three and a half years (this is a close estimate from the Bible scholars) to turn the world upside down. That should encourage you that when God releases you, it will not take God long to do the work.

No matter how long you have been waiting, there is still time for you to fulfill your purpose on this earth. Don't feel like you are too old or too young for that matter. God wants to use you, and He has called you to do a work. God has given you those gifts and talents to bless His people. You are a gift, in fact, as it states in Ephesians 4:8–16. Each of us have been given a measure of faith as it says in Romans 12:3. Although we have been given gifts, sometimes God has us in training, and the gift seems to be dormant. While you are waiting, don't let the enemy lie to you, telling you that you have nothing to offer. God is just refining you during this waiting period. He is making you better than before. You will be like Job who lost everything only to get it all back in a double portion. *What looks like a detour to you now will turn out to be the greatest blessing God could have bestowed upon you.*

Stay Close to God While Waiting

In Isaiah 40:31, it tells us, "They that wait upon the Lord shall renew their strength." While you are waiting on God, expect Him to renew your strength. Tell Him how you really feel. Be honest with God. Remember, God said of David that he was a man after God's own heart, with all his faults, he knew how to humble himself.

One example of the humility seen in David that we need to exemplify was when the Prophet Nathan came to him in 2 Samuel 12:1–7. For those that might not know what happened, it is recorded in 2 Samuel 11 where David took another man's (Uriah) wife (Bathsheba) while that man was out fighting in a battle. Bathsheba became pregnant, and David arranged it so that her husband could be killed in battle, after which, David took Bathsheba to be his wife. When the Prophet Nathan came to check David about it, instead of David becoming arrogant (because after all he was the king), he humbled himself and admitted that he had sinned. David also wrote a couple of Psalms where it is believed he was pouring out his heart due to the Bathsheba incident (a couple of them are Psalm 32 and Psalm 51).

I brought up David because we need to see what it looks like to truly humble ourselves so that God can say of you and I, there's my daughter or my son *seeking after my heart*. Learn how to be transparent with Father God. He already knows you. He saw what you did last night. He knows your thoughts and guess what, He still loves you and wants to use you. He did not call us because we were perfect vessels. In fact, God seems to prefer to use cracked, broken vessels so that His glory can be seen. If we had it all together, we would not be of any use to God, because we would feel we did not need Him. Remember the words to the old hymn that should help keep us grounded:

> My hope is built on nothing less than Jesus Christ, my righteousness, I dare not trust the sweetest frame, but wholly lean on Jesus name, On Christ the solid Rock I stand, all other ground is sinking sand.

While we are waiting before Him, we will see some ugly things about ourselves. Maybe some flaws we thought we had overcome long ago. Just remember, He is refining us, and this pause, detour, or waiting period is just to refine you even more so that when you emerge from this place, you will shine like a precious stone, and you will come out as refined gold. James tells us, "No chastening at the time seems joyous, but afterward the chastening and refining of my Father will yield the peaceable fruits of righteousness." In other words, this situation is helping me to be made more like Him.

The truth of the matter is neither you nor I know what it will take to bring us to perfection or make us into vessels that He can use. God loves us so much that He has chosen us and decided that He wants to use us for His glory. Yes, God is God, and He could very well do it without us, but He has decided to co-labor with us.

What an honor to be used by Him. What an honor to be called by Him! Life for us is just starting. The waiting, the pain, the trials, and the tests are nothing compared to the glory that He shall reveal in us!

Our journey is just beginning, so let us not grow weary in well-doing; for in due season, we shall reap if we faint not. Dr. Martin Luther King Jr. saw something that convinced him that it did not matter what they did to him for he said, "Mine eyes have seen the glory." What are we looking at? We need to turn our eyes on Him (God) so that we can behold His glory. The scriptures tell us that eye hath not seen, ear hath not heard all that God has prepared for them that love Him, but God has revealed them to us through His spirit (1 Corinthians 2:9).

We have a race to run, and there might be trouble ahead. There will be good days, but there will also be some hills to climb. There will be times when you will shed some tears. But as the Apostle Paul said, "This one thing I do, forgetting those things that are behind, I press toward the mark for the prize of the high calling in God in Christ Jesus" (Philippians 3:13–14).

This world is not your home; remember, you are just passing through. Have you ever noticed how you don't seem to fit in? That's because we are just passing through here. This is not our final resting place. We are in this world, but we are not of this world. These are exciting times if you can see it. God is doing a great work in you while you wait on Him.

> Nugget: *What looks like a detour to you now will turn out to be the greatest blessing God could have bestowed upon you.*

Chapter 6

Forgiveness

One thing that can hinder us is when we have unforgiveness in our hearts. This is a big one for most of us. The truth of the matter is that while we are on this earth, someone will offend us or hurt our feelings at one time or another. Unforgiveness is not an option. We are commanded to forgive one another as stated in Matthew 18:21–22, "Then Peter came to Jesus and asked, 'Lord, how many times shall I forgive my brother or sister who sins against me? Up to seven times?' Jesus answered, 'I tell you, not seven times, but seventy-seven times.'"

Notice this verse from the NIV version indicates seventy-seven (77) times. I have seen other translations that said seventy times seven (490) times. I believe the point Jesus is making is that you are to continue to forgive no matter how many times people offend you. Let's be real, it is not easy to forgive.

In Matthew 6:12 (NKJV), in the sermon on the mount, the prayer is, "…Forgive us our debts (faults) as we forgive our debtors (faults)." According to that scripture, you being forgiven depends on whether you forgive others. In verses fourteen and fifteen of this same chapter, Jesus said it very plainly that if we forgive others their trespasses, our heavenly Father will forgive us. But if we forgive not others their trespasses, *neither will our Father forgive our trespasses!* Anyone reading this who's struggling with forgiving someone and can't seem to let it go, please read *Matthew 6: 12–15*.

You are on dangerous ground if you refuse to forgive someone who has hurt you.

Believe me I get it! I've been there when someone hurts you so badly that you literally feel like they just took a knife and stabbed you in the heart. God showed me that He had so much more in store for me. I had to choose whether I would continue to be mad, bitter, hurt, and upset, or was I going to trust God to work it out and forgive by faith. I had to choose between staying stuck where I was and playing the situation over and over again in my mind (which makes us get mad all over again) or to let it go and enter a deeper realm with God. It was hard, but through tears, I chose to let it go and move on in God.

You, my friend, will have to do the same if you want what God has for you. Don't wait until you *feel like it.* Say you forgive them by faith. I said, "Lord, I don't want to forgive this person, but I know that You require that we continue to forgive no matter how many times we get offended, so, God, I speak it by faith and ask you to help me mean it in my heart." In all honesty, you never forget what the person did to you, but it becomes less and less painful. Eventually, you find that you have let it go.

Colossians 3:12–13 reads as follows, "Therefore, as God's chosen people, holy and dearly loved, clothe yourselves with compassion, kindness, humility, gentleness and patience. Bear with each other and forgive one another if any of you has a grievance against someone. Forgive as the Lord forgave you."

This verse in Colossians tells us that we need to clothe ourselves with compassion, kindness, humility, gentleness, and patience. To clothe yourself means you put it on; you wear it all the time. We are commanded here again to forgive as we have been forgiven. This is not a request. It is a command. We must forgive.

I love the way the New Living Translation records verse thirteen as follows, "*Make allowance for each other's faults and forgive anyone who offends you. Remember, the Lord forgave you, so you must forgive others.*"

When it says make allowance, that means that we should expect that while we are living on this earth, someone is going to offend us. In fact, we will be dealing with offenses until Jesus comes back just because we are not perfect, and we are dealing with imperfect people. Just remember, you have probably offended someone before as well. Sometime ago, a member of our church came to me and informed me that I had offended her by something I said. I was literally shocked, because I had no clue that she was offended. But when she reminded me of what I said, I could see how she could have been offended. I felt bad, because I truly did not mean it the way she took it. I apologized to her and told her that I was sorry that I had offended her, because that was not my intention.

If someone comes to you because they feel you offended them, please don't belittle them or make light of it, or think, *Well they should get tougher skin*. No, no, no. You should sincerely apologize even if you can't see how what you did or said offended them. The goal is to clear the air and give no place for the devil to bring division or discord. Read Matthew 18:15–17 (NKJV) to learn how you deal with Christians in the church in resolving offenses. Briefly: You go to that person first to talk about it. If they will not listen, go back again, and take a witness with you. If they still refuse to hear you, meet with them and the pastor (church). If that person still refuses to reconcile, you are done. The Bible had some strong words to say about that person at that point. Move on, and make sure you pray for that person. Because you did your part, and their issue is now with God.

In Matthew 5:23–24, it reads, "Therefore, if you are offering your gift at the altar and there remember that your brother or sister has something against you, leave your gift there in front of the altar. First go and be reconciled to them; then come and offer your gift."

Some of our prayers might not be getting answered if we have not resolved some situations. Basically, this is saying that if you are praying and remember that there is an unresolved matter, you need to go and ask for forgiveness, or forgive them. Make the situation right so that your prayers are not hindered.

In 1 John 3:15, it reads, "Anyone who hates a brother or sister is a murderer, and you know that no murderer has eternal life residing in him." I pray that no one has allowed unforgiveness to get so deep in their soul that it has turned to hate. We never fall too deep where

God cannot find us. If you do find that you are in a place where you feel like it could be hatred that you are feeling, it is not too late for you to get out of that pit.

Pause and pray to God right here and right now as follows,

> Father God, You already know my thoughts and my heart. You know how I feel about _____. I'm asking You right now to cleanse me of this hate and allow me to love this person like You love them, unconditionally. I repent for any bad thoughts I have had about this person, and I ask you to forgive me and set me free today. Amen!

In Luke 17:1, Jesus said to his disciples, "Things that cause people to stumble are bound to come, but woe to anyone through whom they come." In the King James Version, this verse reads, "…It is impossible but that offenses will come, but woe unto him, through whom they come!" This verse is telling us that you do not want to be the one going around offending everybody with your words or with your actions. Shame on you if you have no control over your tongue and intentionally say things to hurt people. The Bible says, "*Woe unto you!*"

Don't think for one minute the person who offended you will get away with it. God said in Romans 12:19, "*Vengeance is mine, I will repay, saith the Lord*". God has your back. We should be afraid to mess with God's people. As a parent, how do you feel when someone offends your child? We get all protective, and depending on the level of the offense, we are ready to fight (physically) for our children. Well, God is the same way. "He that touches you touches the apple of His eye" (Zechariah 2:8)! "He keeps every tear we shed in a bottle" (Psalms 56:8). God will always vindicate us in His time. I have literally seen the ruin of people who had intentionally did me wrong. I even recalled one incident where I knew God's judgement was about to fall on someone who did me wrong, and I prayed for the person, because I just knew something was about to happen to them. Believe me, God can take care of your enemies better than you can.

If the person you offended or who offended you has passed away, you can still make that situation right in your heart with God. You can still forgive them even if they are now in their grave. You can also ask God to forgive you if you are the one who offended them. It is not too late to make things right in your heart. We need to release all those hurt feelings, because they hold us down, and *we need to soar*!

Before we leave this topic on forgiveness, there is just one more thing we need to address. We must watch our attitude when we have been wronged. There will always be the temptation of wanting something bad to happen to the person. We are called to be like Jesus who said, "Father forgive them for they know not what they do."

> Nugget: *If this offense or situation you are in is causing you to cry out to God, if it is driving you to your knees, then it is doing what it is meant to do*!

Chapter 7

Sin and the Gray Areas

God is coming back for a church without spot or wrinkle or any other blemishes. He is coming back for his bride (us). We want to be ready when Jesus returns which means we must allow God to cleanse us from everything that is not like Him.

In Hebrews 12:1–3 it reads,

> Therefore, since we are surrounded by such a great cloud of witnesses, let us throw off everything that hinders and the sin that so easily entangles. And let us run with perseverance the race marked out for us, fixing our eyes on Jesus, the pioneer and perfecter of faith. For the joy set before him he endured the cross, scorning its shame, and sat down at the right hand of the throne of God. Consider him who endured such opposition from sinners, so that you will not grow weary and lose heart.

This chapter follows the heroes of faith in "Chapter Eleven." They are the cloud of witnesses this verse is referring to. Those that have gone on before are waiting on us. We must not entangle ourselves with weights, sins, or the gray areas (those things *not* specifically spelled out in the scriptures that people like to debate about, whether it is wrong or right for a Christian to do).

Our flesh is prone to sin, that is why we must reckon our flesh to be dead and not allow it to rule us. Most of us do not like to deny our flesh of anything (overeating, sex, excessive alcohol, excessive shopping, etc.). You get the picture: anything in excess is not good for us.

In 1 Corinthians 6:12–20 it reads,

> "I have the right to do anything," you say—but not everything is beneficial. "I have the right to do anything"—but I will not be mastered by anything…" The body, however, is not meant for sexual immorality but for the Lord, and the Lord for the body. By his power God raised the Lord from the dead, and he will raise us also. Do you not know that your bodies are members of Christ himself? Shall I then take the members of Christ and unite them with a prostitute? Never! Do you not know that he who unites himself with a prostitute is one with her in body? For it is said, "The two will become one flesh." But whoever is united with the Lord is one with him in spirit.
>
> Flee from sexual immorality. All other sins a person commits are outside the body, but whoever sins sexually, sins against their own body. Do you not know that your bodies are temples of the Holy Spirit, who is in you, whom you have received from God? You are not your own; you were bought at a price. Therefore, honor God with your bodies.

There are some *obvious sins* that we clearly recognize as sin such as fornication (having sex before you get married), adultery (married people having sex with someone who is not his/her spouse), lying, stealing, etc. Of course, the Ten Commandments give us a picture of what we should or should not be doing. We should all agree that we should not engage in the *obvious sins.*

Let's see what the Bible says about sin. In Revelation 21:8, it gives us a more detailed list of who will go to hell: the fearful, unbelievers, the abominable (hateful), murderers, whoremongers (sexual sins), sorcerers (a witch or using witchcraft), idolaters (worshiping idols), and liars. Doesn't it seem strange to you that God added liars to this list? According to *Webster*, the definition of lying is *to make an untrue statement with the intent to deceive.* So if you say, "The event starts at 4:00 p.m.," and you find out later it actually was supposed to start at 5:00 p.m., you did not lie. You were mistaken. However, if you had the invitation in your hand and you knew it said 5:00 p.m., and you purposely said it starts at 4:00 p.m., you are lying.

I was shocked when I found out as a young Christian that some professing Christians lie on a regular basis. My mother raised us to believe that lying was the worst thing you could possibly do. Growing up with eleven other siblings, when my mom would line us up (I am referring to the younger six children as the older ones were grown), and say, for example, "Who stole the cookies?" She would follow her question up with, "If I find out you are lying to me, you will be in trouble for stealing the cookies and then you are going to get it for lying to me." She used to always tell us with all the seriousness she had in her, "A liar will not tarry in His sight!" Back then, we did not know what all that meant except that it was serious, and we better not lie to her. That being said, *I am sure we have all told a lie before.*

God knows we are not perfect, but a lie is just like any other sin. If you tell a lie, you should be convicted and ask God to forgive you. Remember, the Bible says, "All liars will have their part in the lake that burns with fire." As Christians, lying should not be the norm for us. If we lie (sin), we have an advocate (Jesus) who has died for our sins. But if you are comfortable with lying (saying things that you *know* are not true), and you are lying every day, you are what they call *practicing sin.* Christians who represent Christ, should not be liars. If this is you, ask God to help you in that area. You wouldn't want your lying to keep you out of the kingdom. Read the scripture for yourself in Revelations 21:8. All liars will be thrown into the lake of fire. The truth is that Jesus could come back any day now. We need to make sure our lives are in order.

I must tell you the truth, and what the Bible says about sin, because I don't want you to be deceived into thinking you are okay. I want to see you in heaven. Let's look at one more list in the Bible of people who will not be going to heaven. This list is found in 1 Corinthians 6:9–10: the unrighteous, fornicators, idolaters, adulterers, effeminate (homosexuals), sodomites (having anal or oral sex), thieves, covetous, drunkards, revilers (saying evil things about people), extortioners (blackmailing people). I did not make up this list! Read it for yourself! I am only the messenger telling you what the word of God says.

Thank God for Jesus! I think we were all somewhere in that list before Jesus saved us. Now that he has washed us in his blood and made us clean, we are no longer practicing the things in the above noted lists (1 Corinthians 6:11). For those who can still find yourself practicing the above noted list of sins, it is not too late for you. In fact, you are reading this book because God is trying to get your attention. He loves you so much no matter what you have done or where you have been. Please do not take this as if I am judging you. No, I am pleading with you, because I want to see you in heaven. *All* have sinned and fallen short of the glory of God. No one is better than anyone else. The difference is some of us have come to the realization that *we need Jesus*.

If you have never accepted Jesus into your heart (salvation), no time is better than the present time. Jesus is calling you right now. It is not His will that any of us should go to hell. Hell was not even created for us. It was created for the devil and his demons. I am pleading with you, because tomorrow is not promised to any of us, choose Him today. I guarantee you, it will be the best thing that ever happened to you. He will turn your life around and fix everything that has been broken.

You have tried everything else; why not give Jesus a try. Go back to "Chapter Three" of this book and follow those simple steps on how to be saved. Jesus can save you anywhere: at home, at church, in the hospital; God is not limited by our protocols. He can do what

He wants, when, and where He wants to do it. After you do the sinner's prayer found in "Chapter Three," ask God to lead you to a good Bible-believing church where you can grow in Him.

We have discussed the obvious sins; now let's talk about the *gray areas* that Christians like to argue about, because they are not clearly stated in the Bible as sin. This would include things such as smoking, drinking, gambling, etc.

As a Christian, you belong to Jesus, and you cannot do whatever you want to do to your body (His temple). In the scripture above (1 Corinthians 6:12), it tells us, "We may be free to do anything (gray areas), but everything is not good for us to do (my translation)." *We should not overdo anything.* Follow the leading of the Holy Spirit. For those that might not know what I mean: the Holy Spirit will give us a little nudge when we are about to do something God does not want us to do. I find that the Holy Spirit does His job in pulling our coattail, but we don't always like to listen to the nudge, and we do it anyway. The more you ignore the Holy Spirit, the easier it will be to do that thing again (overeat, lie, get drunk, etc.).

Often, people say, if the Bible does not specifically say it is a sin, I'm okay with it. Smoking will destroy your lungs. Drugs will affect your brain. Overeating will lead to obesity and a lot of other health issues. If what you are engaging in will have a negative effect on your body, you should not be doing it. You are defiling His temple (which is your body). An addiction to gambling could eventually bring your entire household to financial ruin (I'm speaking of those who have no self-control and end up using rent money or other bill money to gamble).

Because God is cleansing us, don't get discouraged when he shows you something about yourself that needs to change (bad temper, no patience, laziness, stubbornness, overeating, lust, excessive drinking, or anything you are overdoing). Just know that we are all *a work in progress,* and God is not finished with us yet!

> Nugget: *Nothing impure will enter heaven! Now is the time for us to let God cleanse and purify us so that we can enter those gates boldly* (Revelation 21:27).

CHAPTER 8

Your Gifts and Talents Are Needed

In Ephesians 4:11–13, we are told that God gave gifts to the Church to be used to bring us into the unity of the faith and the knowledge of the Son of God until we reach perfection in Christ. That is my abbreviated version of those scriptures.

In Romans 12:3–8, it reads,

> For by the grace given me I say to every one of you: Do not think of yourself more highly than you ought, but rather think of yourself with sober judgment, in accordance with the faith God has distributed to each of you. For just as each of us has one body with many members, and these members do not all have the same function, so in Christ we, though many, form one body, and each member belongs to all the others. We have different gifts, according to the grace given to each of us. If your gift is prophesying, then prophesy in accordance with your faith; if it is serving, then serve; if it is teaching, then teach; if it is to encourage, then give encouragement; if it is giving, then give generously; if it is to lead, do it diligently; if it is to show mercy, do it cheerfully.

The body of Christ needs the gift that God has given you. If you do not do your part, something will be missing. Often, people will sit on their gifts because they feel that someone else can do it better. You are robbing us when you do that. Whatever your gift is, no one can do it like you! God has gifted you to build up His kingdom. So what are you doing with your gift?

There is a parable in the Bible about a person who was given a talent and did not use it (Matthew 25:14–30). As a result of not using his talent, it was taken away from him. God gave me an example of what happens when we do not use the gifts He has given us. Think about what happens with the muscles in our body if we do not use them. For instance, if we were bedridden and never used our legs, eventually we would experience *muscle atrophy* (when your muscles waste away to the point where you are unable to use them). We must continue to use our muscles and to exercise if we want to have healthy muscles. It is the same with our gifts and talents. If we never use them, eventually, we will be unable to use them. Just as we use our natural muscles to prevent them from wasting away (muscle atrophy), we also must use our spiritual muscles (the gifts and talents God gave to each of us) to prevent them from wasting away due to lack of use.

It is also a bad idea to compare yourself to others. God made us different for a reason. He seems to like variety. Just like no two people have the same fingerprints, no two people have the exact same expression. When God decided to use you and give you that gift, He knew that it went well with your personality. For example, one of my gifts is teaching. When I teach, I have noticed that my personality comes out as I teach. It is the same for all other teachers; they have a certain style that is a characteristic of them.

Some people say they don't know what their gift is. To give you a hint, you can usually spot your gift because it is that thing that you love to do, and you would rather be doing that than anything else. For example, if you like to entertain and feed people, you probably have the gift of hospitality. If you like to set things in order and you are good at organizing events, etc., you probably have the gift of administration. If God frequently reveals a person's heart to you and when you share it with them you are usually right on, you probably have a prophetic gift, etc. I think you get the point.

Read 1 Corinthians 12:12–27. Here, Paul reminds us that we are one body and many members. We don't realize how much we depend on our natural body to function properly until one of our parts malfunctions. For example, a couple of years ago, I had an episode with my vision. Suddenly, everything became blurry. I had to stop working on my computer, put compresses on my eyes, and lay down on the couch in my office at work with the door locked until my eyes recovered. That was a bit scary for me, and I began to pray, because I still would have to drive home. Thank God allowing my eyes to rest took care of the problem. Up until that moment, I took my eyes for granted. Not anymore! I was told I have dry eyes and that was the cause of my problem, so now I faithfully use drops to keep my eyes lubricated, because I need them functioning properly.

We need all our parts to function properly. "The eye cannot say to the hand, 'I don't need you!' And the head cannot say to the feet, 'I don't need you' (verse twenty-one)! Our natural body is a type of our spiritual body. We need what you have to offer; without you, the body is not whole. Something is missing!

Just one more thing about the gifts: when you have a gift, eventually everyone will see it and know it. Your gift will make room for you (Proverbs 18:16). This means there is a place for you in the body of Christ.

> Nugget: *Get in your rightful place! We need you! There is only one of you, and nobody can do it or say it like you! So take that gift off the shelf, dust it off, and start using it for the kingdom.*

Chapter 9

Love Your Neighbor as You Love Yourself

God is love. If we are His offspring, people should see His love in us. In Matthew 22:36–40, it reads,

> "Teacher, which is the greatest commandment in the Law?"
> Jesus replied: "Love the Lord your God with all your heart and with all your soul and with all your mind." This is the first and greatest commandment. And the second is like it: "Love your neighbor as yourself." All the Law and the Prophets hang on these two commandments.

Truth be told, we don't really have a hard time with the First Great Commandment. We are so in love with God! If that was all that was required of us, we would be okay (smile). We want to address the Second Great Commandment: *Love your neighbor as you love yourself.* How much do we love ourselves? It seems to me that if you have not learned to love yourself, it will be impossible for you to love your neighbor.

Say what you want, but if we really loved ourselves the way we should, we would take better care of our bodies. I am not pointing the finger at you. I am just as guilty of neglecting myself. I was listening to Joyce Meyers the other day (who is seventy-five years old and she looks great), and she was encouraging the congregation to get their proper rest and drink plenty of water. She went on to say that some of you think you have all these deep problems and feel like you need to have hours of counseling about your problems, and she said, "All you really need to do is *get some sleep and drink some water.*" She had us all laughing. But you know, there is some truth to what she said.

I'm on a *better me* journey. Let me just say, I *love to eat*! I don't just eat when I am hungry; I eat because I see it there, and the cake or cookies are always calling my name. I am a little embarrassed to type this, but I think if we really want to change our ways, we need to be real with ourselves. Some of us need to start exercising some tough love on ourselves. I challenge you to go to your bathroom, take off all your clothes, and look in the mirror at yourself. If you are happy with what you see then this does not apply to you, but if you are looking at a protruding stomach, love handles, etc., it is time to make a change. Time for you to *love you more*!

You would be surprised at what a difference small changes make. I have been on my better me journey for the past three weeks, and I have lost ten pounds. It's not always easy, but it's something I know God wants me to do. One of the fruits of the spirit that is supposed to be working for us is *self-control* (Galatians 5:22-23). I think we must have buried that fruit of the spirit. We all have the fruit of self-control. Stir up the gift in us, Lord!

We owe it to ourselves, our children, and our grandchildren (if we are old enough to be a grandparent) to take better care of ourselves. Obesity opens the door for all kinds of health issues. We know what we need to do to get in shape. A few things I have done is to drink more water (I am drinking four sixteen-ounce bottles a day which is still less than what is recommended for me). I try to walk (brisk walk) at least thirty minutes—five days a week (I either walk around the park or if the weather is bad, I walk at the mall in the morning with the senior citizens before the mall opens). I limit fried foods (I probably should cut them out completely, but every once in a while, I want some fried chicken or fish). I limit my carb intake and sweets (bread, rice, potatoes, cake, ice cream, etc.). I also eat a lot more fruits and vegetables now.

Some days are better than other days. Eating right needs to be our new lifestyle. So even if we mess up and fall off for a day, the next day, we should get right back on track. Each day is a new day, and we can always start all over again. Just remember, these are the only bodies we are going to get here on this earth, so we better take good care of them (we will not get our glorified body until Christ returns).

Oh, I do understand about comfort eating or stress eating. Don't do it! Find other ways to deal with the stress of the day (pray; get your praise on). Grab an apple instead of those cookies.

We must realize that on this journey back to God, we are going to make some mistakes, and every day will not be perfect. But remember the song that says, "We fall down, but we get up." Every time you fall or do something wrong, brush yourself off and get back up again. It is okay! Someone preached once that there is no shame in falling; the shame is when you don't get back up again.

You are fearfully and wonderfully made (Psalm 139:14). You are beautiful! There is only one of you on this earth. There might be some things we need to tighten up, but God made us beautiful! Start loving on yourself by taking better care of you.

Now I need you to go and look in the mirror and say, *"I love me some you, and from now on, I am going to treat you better and take better care of you."*

Because we have resolved to love ourselves, we can begin to love others. The reason all the law and the prophets are based on us loving God with all our heart and loving our neighbor as ourselves is because if we love God, we will not want to grieve Him by worshiping other gods, making idols, or taking His name in vain. Because we love God, we will honor our parents and remember the Sabbath. When we love our neighbors as we love ourselves, we will not steal from one another, and we will not kill one another. If we truly loved each other, we would not covet what our neighbor has or commit adultery with our neighbor's husband or wife. If we truly loved each other, we would not tell lies about each other.

Love *can be felt*. When people come to visit your church, are they feeling the love, or do they feel strife and disunity? I tell you the truth: if people do not feel the love when they visit your church, they probably will not be back. I remember about twenty or so years ago, I was looking for a church home. I had visited several churches but had not gotten that witness that this is the one. At last, I went to a church, and when I walked in the door, the only way I can explain it was that it felt like someone had made a nice cozy fire, and we were all huddled around it. It felt so warm and fuzzy, and I knew I was home.

We are commanded to love one another. People know that we belong to Him, because they see the love we have for each other (John 13:35). God put so much importance on us loving each other that we have an entire chapter in 1 Corinthians 13 where Paul tells us, "You can prophesy, speak in other tongues, have the gift of knowledge, be a giver, have faith to move mountains, and have suffered greatly, yet if you don't have love, none of that matters."

In 1 Corinthians 13:4–8 it gives us the best description in the Bible of what true love looks like:

> Love is patient, love is kind. It does not envy, it does not boast, it is not proud. It does not dishonor others, it is not self-seeking, it is not easily angered, it keeps no record of wrongs. Love does not delight in evil but rejoices with the truth. It always protects, always trusts, always hopes, always perseveres. Love never fails.

I particularly like the part where it says, "*Love keeps no record of wrongs...*" Some of us better throw out some file cabinets!!!!! We have been keeping records of wrongs (in our minds) for years. Ask God to help you to display the kind of love that keeps no record of wrongs done to you.

I know we must work on this love thing. There is no compromising here. God is love, and we are supposed to be like Him. Maybe it is not as hard as we think to love one another. We just need to put on the mind of Christ, and we will see each other the way God sees us. Perhaps we need to stop looking at each other's actions and see the heart as God does. A person could be attacking you verbally, but their heart is crying out, *Please help me. I don't want to be like this.*

Jesus was able to look beyond the fault and see the need. He has called us to do the same. Love covers a multitude of sins (1 Peter 4:8). It is time to stop hating on each other, and let the love flow!

> Nugget: *The love of God is already in us (because God is in us); we just need to open our hearts and let the love flow.*

Chapter 10

Spiritual Warfare

If we expect to be victorious in this life, we must recognize that we have a real enemy, Satan, and all the demons that work with him. Their sole purpose is to keep you and I from reaching our destiny by any means necessary. Someone once said that the best thing the devil could have done was to convince people that he does not exist. That was wise on his part. Look at all the havoc he could cause and not be blamed for it. His tactics are the same: he whispers something in your ear about someone and whispers in their ear about you, and before you know it, you are arguing and fighting with each other, and he sits back and laughs.

We need to wake up and realize that our fight is not with each other. We are on the same team. Ephesians 6:12 tells us, "For our struggle is not against flesh and blood, but against the rulers, against the authorities, against the powers of this dark world and against the spiritual forces of evil in the heavenly realms."

Because we have an enemy, we need to remember that every thought that comes to our head is not necessarily our thought. Someone gave an example once that you can't stop the birds from landing on your head, but you do not have to let them make a nest there. What that means is you can't stop a thought from coming to your mind, but you sure don't have to keep dwelling on that thought after it comes. Learn how to dismiss thoughts. The enemy puts a thought in our mind, and before we realize it, we have made a motion picture out of that one thought, because we continued to think about it and added more to it.

We live in a promiscuous society. The enemy has deceived a lot of our young people into thinking that just because they might have experimented with the same sex, they now must change their identity. That's a trick of the enemy. You are who God says you are. Fornication (sex before marriage) is a sin whether it is with the opposite sex or the same sex. The devil tempts us; we fall then he laughs at us and try to condemn us. Remember, we have all sinned and fallen short of the glory of God. None of us can point our fingers at the other. God loves us no matter what we have done, and He is always waiting for us to just repent and run to Him. We all need Jesus to help us fight this spiritual warfare we find ourselves in daily. Satan will continually try to ensnare us any way he can. We must recognize his tactics, resist him, and watch him flee from us.

Most of our battles take place and start in our minds. That is why in 1 Peter 1:13, we are told to "…gird up the loins of your mind." Other translations say, "Prepare your minds for action."

In 1 Peter 5:8 it reads: "Be alert and of sober mind. Your enemy the devil prowls around like a roaring lion looking for someone to devour." Again, here we see the scriptures warn us to be alert and sober in our minds because of our enemy. If the devil can get into your head and get you to doubt and question God, he is being successful. Look what he did to Eve. He got into her head and made her question God's command. Our thoughts can get us into trouble if we are not careful. Has someone ever made you upset, and, after a while, you thought you were over it? But once you start thinking about it, you got mad all over again.

If we want to stay free, we must stop playing some of the tapes that we have been listening to in our minds. I'm referring to when you keep on thinking about the wrong that was done to you, and you can't seem to get over it. It plays over and over again in your head. Until you stop playing that tape, you will not be free of that person or situation. Harboring bitterness and resentment in our hearts keeps the door open for the devil to continue to torment us in that area. When you make up your mind that you don't want to live there anymore, and you stop playing those *what-they-did-to-me tapes*, you will find so much more peace and freedom in your life. If we refuse to let it go, it will become like a weight that is holding us down and keeping us from soaring in the heavenlies with God.

So we need to gird up our minds. How do we gird up our minds? Refuse to listen to negative thoughts. When they come, for they will come, we need to rebuke those thoughts quickly. We must cause our mind to think on the things listed in Philippians 4:8,

> Finally, brothers and sisters, whatever is true, whatever is noble, whatever is right, whatever is pure, whatever is lovely, whatever is admirable, if anything is excellent or praiseworthy, think about such things.

Verse seven of that same chapter speaks of the peace of God that will *guard* our hearts and *minds*. We must realize that our minds need to be guarded as well as our hearts.

Sometimes it is difficult to turn the thoughts off. There are times when we feel like we are being flooded with thoughts. At times like that, the scripture says, "When the enemy comes in like a flood, the spirit of God will lift up a standard against him" (Isaiah 59:19, KJV). In other words, those times when we just can't seem to shake it are the times when we need to call on the name of Jesus. After you call upon Jesus's name, watch how he causes all the voices to cease and brings the peace that only He can bring. When we are under attack, it is much like the ship that was being tossed in the Bible, and Jesus was called upon to stop the storm. He simply said, "Peace be still and the winds and waves obeyed Him" (Mark 4:39). We don't have to fight our battles alone. Remember, we have help if we just call upon Him.

Even while writing this section of the book, God allowed me to see how subtle the enemy is. Remember, his main goal is to get us *distracted* so that we do not reach our destiny. I received a phone call while writing this section from someone who was genuinely concerned for me, and it caused me to question some things the Lord had spoken to me. I became sidetracked thinking about what was said. When you love the Lord, you always want to make sure you are hearing Him correctly and that you are doing His perfect will. We must trust that if God said He would lead us and guide us, He meant just that. We need to stop stressing about if we are on the right track or not. God wants to get us there (back to Him) more than we want to get there. We don't always understand our journey or the path He takes us down, but there is freedom in knowing that God said He would work all things out for our good.

I have always believed that God loves us so much that even if we get deceived for a moment, God will bring us out of that deception. Think about it. He knows your heart, and if you are continually crying out to know Him, He is going to get you there no matter how many detours you go down. Someone explained it like this to me once: open your hand and point to and find a center point on your palm. Now start at the tip of each one of your fingers (envision each finger is a road that leads you to the palm of your hand) and draw a line from the tip of each finger to that center point. With each finger you follow, you will still get to that central point. In other words, when you are a child of God, you must believe that the path of the just *is as a shining light*. Although some routes might be quicker or shorter, you will end up just where God wants you to be, because you belong to Him, and He said He would *never leave you or forsake you*.

We are going to take a detour here for just a moment. I feel I need to share a little of my testimony with you. I came to the Lord when I was fourteen years old. As I look back on my life, God was calling me way before I turned fourteen. Don't laugh. But when I was growing up, every Easter and Christmas, when they would play all the good Christian movies (*King of Kings, the Ten Commandments*, etc.), I would become convicted and weep and decide that I wanted to be saved and follow Jesus. That would last about two weeks, and then I would change my mind and decide I'm not ready yet. Thank God for raising me in a Christian home.

My dad was a preacher and had his own church for a while. My mom was also saved when she was fourteen years old, and she loved the Lord with all her heart. But during one of my *come to Jesus moments*, my mom told me, "Linda, you don't play with God. If you are going to serve Him, you have to mean it." I must have been around ten or eleven years old, and, although I felt I meant it, every year (at least for two weeks out of the year), I decided I wasn't ready, and I did not officially give my life to Him until I turned fourteen. Even at the age of fourteen, when I began living like I belonged to Him, there were some concerned neighbors that told my mother they thought I was too young to be living a saved life.

At age twenty-four, I got mad at God, because I did not like the way my life was going. I wanted to be married (as most Christian girls do because you want to do things the right way). By age twenty-four, I had had two almost-proposals from two different guys, but neither relationship worked out. Finally, at age twenty-four (I had been walking with the Lord for ten years now), I decided that I did not like the way God was doing things, and I felt I could do better on my own without living this saved life.

So at age twenty-four, I officially became a *backslider*. I did not want any parts of God or the Church. I refused to even go to Church, because I knew if I went, something would prick my heart, and I was not ready to feel any conviction. I wanted to do my own thing, because I was under the deception that I could do it better than God. From age twenty-four to age thirty-four (ten years), I did everything I thought I wanted to do. I partied, I dated, and even got married (lasted one year), and divorced. I had a beautiful daughter from my first marriage (I was twenty-nine when I had her). To be honest with you, I could never totally drown God out. He was always there just waiting for me to open the door for Him. I am so grateful to Him, because I know that He was watching over me even while I was in my rebellious state. Things started to turn for me at age thirty. I was still living in sin (cohabitating with my new boyfriend). I had used my general secretary certificate (one year of training) to land a great job. However, to advance at that same job, I decided to go back to school to get my bachelor's degree (obtaining that degree in 1997 enabled me to receive several promotions over the twenty-nine years I worked at the agency. God was good to me!).

But at the age of thirty-four, I began to listen just a little to the tugging in my heart by the Lord. I began to miss the conversations I used to have with the Lord. I started remembering and missing what it was like to just sit in His presence. During this time, when God was softening my heart, a coworker said to me (God can use anyone He pleases to reach us), "What are you doing out here? You know you need to go back to Church." She and I had not been having any discussions about God at that time, so I was shocked when that came out of her mouth. In fact, I asked God why He let her in on our private conversation! I guess I was taking too long listening to that inner voice, so God spoke it to me audibly through someone that I did not want in my business. But guess what, it got my attention, and that next Sunday, I went to Church, and I have been back serving the Lord since that time, and I have not looked back. I was so glad to be back home!

Oh, and the young man that I was cohabitating with is now my husband, David Anderson. We have been married for twenty-five years now. But I must tell you how he became my husband. After the Lord started to deal with me, I knew I had to make things right. I could hear my mother's words ringing in my ears, "You don't play with God. You either live for Him or not. No middle ground." So I gave the talk to my then boyfriend, whom I was living with. I said, "I love you, but it is time for me to get my life right with the Lord and cohabiting is not acceptable to Him. So we will either need to get married or you need to leave, but we cannot continue to live in sin." He agreed that we should get married (many years later, he confessed to me that he thought I would change my mind). Ladies, I was very serious. I had to face the reality when I told him what I had to do; that this man could walk out of my life, and I would be heartbroken and devastated. But the love I had for the Lord had to come first. I had to be willing to be alone and cry into my pillow if need be. Yes, I was so happy when he said we would get married. Subsequently, we had an awesome son who managed to get the best parts of both of us. He is so handsome and smart (sorry, I just got distracted).

I know the Lord had me share that part of my testimony for someone who's on the fence right now, because you are distracted by a man or woman that you think you cannot live without. I don't care what everybody else is doing. You know what God is requiring you to do. God still calls us to *take up our cross and follow Him.* By letting go of those sins that so easily beset us, there is no limit to where you can go in God. God has a blessing with your name on it, but for some of you, you need to stop doing the things you know He is telling you to stop doing. This is between you and God! He wants to take you higher, but you got to let go of all the distractions and things that keep you from going deeper. Your situation might not turn out like mine. Your boyfriend (or girlfriend if you are a guy) could decide to leave you, because you raised your standards. But if he/she leaves, that is only because he/she was not the one for you, and God has something better for you. You will look back on your decision to do it God's way and be so grateful that you did. He's waiting for you! Don't be scared; just do it and trust Him to take care of you!

As I said earlier, if the devil can keep you distracted or sidetracked, he can claim victory. Don't let him do it. Recognize that this thing is just a distraction, and you will not let it hinder you from getting all that God has for you.

Claim Your Home for Jesus

In Joshua 1:3, God told Joshua that everywhere he placed his feet, God had given that land to him. That promise is for us as well. We need to start claiming more territory for Jesus and driving out all spirits and demons that don't belong there. Our homes are a good place to start. You need to do a spiritual house cleaning on your home whenever God places it in your heart to do so. I say it that way, because from time to time, people come into our home and people have baggage. We don't want any bad or negative spirits to linger in our homes. I believe that prayer works whether you go from room to room, pray on your knees for your home, or put anointing oil on the door posts. Let God lead you on how to cleanse your home.

A sample prayer for those that have never had a house cleansing could be,

> Lord, in the name of Jesus I pray for my home. I command anything in my home that is not like You to leave in the name of Jesus. I cover my home and everyone in it with the blood of Jesus. Keep us safe from all hurt, harm, and danger. I pray that any doors we have opened to the enemy, knowingly or unknowingly, be closed in Jesus name. Father, let Your presence and Your peace be felt in our home by anyone who visits. Lord, we dedicate this home to You, knowing that we belong to You as well as our home. Use our home for Your glory. In Jesus's name, amen!

Parents, one or both of you should be laying your hands on your children from time to time to cover them in prayer. My mother, may she rest in peace, would be full of the Holy Spirit from time to time and wake us up out of our sleep as she would have her hand on our head and commence to praying and speaking in other tongues. To be honest, as a child, sometimes my response to her was not nice. I remember a couple of times thinking, *Here she goes again*. But I am convinced that if it wasn't for that warfare prayer of my mother, her twelve kids would not all be saved and would not have become ministers, prophets, teachers, etc. Thank you, Mom, for praying and covering us! You should pray for your children.

One other thing I want to say that my mom did. She told me that when we were each born, she gave us back to the Lord. I'm pretty sure that means we were marked (at least that is how we felt)! I think my family was destined to serve God. If you haven't already done so, give your children back to the Lord.

Here is a prayer you can use, "Lord, You gave these children to me, and I give them back to You to be used for Your glory".

I know the above is not the normal *spiritual warfare* conversation you would expect to have, but I had to go the route God led me to speak on. There are a number of books out there on spiritual warfare that deals with casting out demons, etc. I believe God had me go this route, because if we rebuke the devil in his early stages (suggestions in our minds), we will not have to worry about him getting a stronghold and it resulting in the need to cast out demons.

> Nugget: *Be alert! The devil will try to stop you or slow you down anyway he can. Always remember, God is greater than the enemy, and <u>God's</u> got your back.*

CHAPTER 11

Judgement Day Is Coming

My son and I have discussions about the Bible all the time. He usually has excellent questions about different topics which results in me searching the scriptures to make sure I am giving him the correct answer. I love his questions, because they cause me to give an answer for what I believe. In 2015, (my son was about sixteen years old) he inquired about the end times, and what would be the sequence of the events spoken of in the Book of Revelation.

Like a lot of other people, I really had not studied the *Book of Revelation*, because it is a profound book. To answer his questions about the judgement day events, I began to read the *Book of Revelation* to put the events noted in order. The following is in no way an attempt to explain the book for I believe that one can only understand the *Book of Revelation* via divine enlightenment from God. My thought is that if we at least know what events are recorded, the Holy Spirit can enlighten us at any time He chooses to let us know the deeper meaning of the noted events.

I pray that after reading this chapter, it will cause you to dig more into the *Book of Revelation*. Consider this chapter as an introduction into the book. I have attempted to draw attention to the *main events* recorded and have listed those events in the order of occurrence given in this book (which was written by the Apostle John).

The first three chapters of *Revelation* deals with God's message to the seven Churches (Ephesus, Smyrna, Pergamon, Thyatira, Sardis, Philadelphia, and Laodicea). We will save that for another study.

We want to focus on the judgement day events. Therefore, we will start in *Revelation* "Chapter 4." In this chapter, the Apostle John saw a vision of God sitting on His throne surrounded by twenty-four elders, crowned and wearing white robes. Lightning and thundering came from the throne. He saw seven lamps representing the seven spirits of God (Isaiah 11: 2 talks about the spirit of the Lord: spirit of wisdom, spirit of understanding, spirit of counsel, spirit of might, spirit of knowledge, and the spirit of the fear of the Lord). He also saw a sea of glass-like crystal before the throne and four living creatures surrounded the throne. One creature looked like a lion, one like a calf, one like an eagle, and one had the face of a man. These creatures praised God continually, and every time they did, the twenty-four elders would cast their crowns before the throne and fall down and worship God.

As God sat on the throne, He had a book in his hand that was sealed with *seven seals*, and the only person who was worthy to open the seals was Jesus, who had been slain. Jesus took the book out of God's hand (Rev. 5:1–7).

The twenty-four elders were also carrying golden bowls full of incense which are the prayers of the Saints. (God is listening. Your prayers are being heard.)

The Lamb of God (Jesus) began to open the seven (7) seals as follows:

1. *First Seal opened* (Rev. 6:1)—The white horse is released representing Christ as a conqueror who conquered Satan.
2. *Second Seal opened* (Rev. 6:3)—The red horse is released to take peace away from the earth by bringing war.
3. *Third Seal opened* (Rev. 6:5)—The black horse is released to bring hunger and famine to the earth.

4. *Fourth Seal opened* (Rev. 6:7)—The pale horse is released to bring death by weapons, famine, and evil men.
5. *Fifth Seal opened* (Rev. 6:9—All the martyrs are seen with their cry to God to avenge them. They were told to rest a little while longer until others are killed the way they were.

    It is believed that we are now living in the time just before the sixth seal is opened.
6. *Sixth Seal opened* (Rev. 6:12)—The opening of this seal brings cosmic disturbances such as earthquakes, the sun becomes black, the moon becomes like blood, the stars of heaven fall from the sky, men hid in caves and wanted the mountain to fall on them, so they could escape the wrath of God.
    a. *Four angels at the four corners of the earth* are ready to harm the earth but are told to wait until the seal of God has been placed in his servants' foreheads (Rev. 7:1).
    b. *The 144,000 were sealed* in their foreheads (Rev. 7:6)
    c. *The rapture takes place* (Rev. 7:9–17)
7. *Seventh Seal opened* (Rev. 8:1–2)—The opening of this seal brought silence in heaven for half an hour in preparation for the trumpets that were coming next. An angel was holding a censer that contained the prayers of the saints. Thunderings, lightning, and an earthquake also occurred at this time.

After the opening of the seals comes seven trumpets sounded by seven angels as follows:

1. *First Trumpet sounded* (Rev. 8:7)—Hail and fire mixed with blood sent on the earth and destroys one third of the earth, one third of the trees, and all the grass is destroyed by fire.
2. *Second Trumpet sounded* (Rev. 8:8)—A great mountain burning with fire is thrown into the sea, and it kills one third of all sea creatures and one third of all ships are destroyed.

3. *Third Trumpet sounded* (Rev. 8:10)—A burning star fell from heaven into the waters and turned one third of the waters bitter. Many men died after drinking the bitter water.
4. *Fourth Trumpet sounded* (Rev. 8:12)—One third of the sun, moon, and stars are struck, and the earth becomes dark.
5. *Fifth Trumpet sounded* (Rev. 9:1)—An angel opened the bottomless pit and released locust (grasshoppers). They were shaped like horses, had teeth like lions, tails like scorpions with stings in them, and they were allowed to hurt men (all those without the seal of God on their foreheads) for five months. Men longed to die to get away from the torment.
6. *Sixth Trumpet sounded* (Rev. 9:13)—The four angels that were prepared for this time were released to kill one third of mankind. It was an army of 200 million demonic-inspired military forces. They destroyed men with fire, smoke, and brimstone. *After witnessing all this, the people that were not killed still refused to repent for their murders, sorceries, sexual immorality, and their thefts.*
    a. *Two Witnesses* were given the power to prophecy for three and a half years. Fire came out of their mouth to kill anyone that tried to harm them. They were also given power to shut up heaven so that it will not rain, turn water into blood, and to strike the earth with plagues as often as they desire (Rev. 11).
    b. At the end of the three and a half years, the beast will kill the witnesses, and they will lay in the street (unburied) for *three and a half days*. After the *three and a half* days, God will breathe life back into them, and they will stand to their feet (with everyone watching and afraid), and God will take the two witnesses to heaven. An earthquake will follow and *kill 7,000 people,* and the rest of the people will be afraid and give glory to God.

7. *Seventh Trumpet sounded* (Rev. 11:15)—The twenty-four elders will then proclaim God's Kingdom. Lightnings, noises, thunderings, an earthquake, and great hail will follow the proclamation.

Events that take place just prior to the Bowls of Wrath being poured out.

I. *Vision seen of a woman who had a child and the dragon tried to kill the child, but the child was caught up to heaven.* So the dragon went after the woman, but he was unable to get to her and she was hidden and fed in the wilderness for *three and a half* years (Rev. 12).

II. *War broke out in heaven, and Satan was cast down to the earth.* He is angry because he knows his time is short (Rev. 12: 7–12). Because he could not get the woman, the beast went to make war with her seed.

III. *A beast rises from the sea (like a leopard)*—(anti-Christ) the dragon gave him authority, and he worshiped the dragon. This beast was granted permission to make war with the saints to overcome them. All whose names are not written in the Book of Life of the Lamb will worship the beast. This beast was wounded (one of his heads) (Rev. 13:1).

IV. *A beast rises from the earth.* This beast was also given authority and forced everyone to worship the beast from the sea. This beast also had power to perform signs (fire from heaven). He killed all those that would not worship the image of the beast. He forces everyone to receive the mark of the beast on their right hand or in their forehead, or they would not be able to buy or sell (number of the beast is 666) (Rev. 13:11).

V. *The 144,000 seen singing a song unto God that only they could sing.* These were those who followed the lamb wherever he went. They were pure (undefiled) and redeemed (Rev. 14:1–5).

VI. *Three angels appear each with a message.*
 1. First angel said fear God and give him glory.
 2. Second angel declared Babylon the great has fallen.
 3. The third angel warned that if the people take the mark of the beast, they will suffer in the lake that burn with fire with the beast forever in torment (Rev. 14: 6–11).

VII. *Sickles thrust into the earth* because it is time to reap the harvest. The grapes were fully ripe (Rev. 14:14).

VIII. *Sea of Glass seen with overcomers playing harps and singing the song of Moses* (Rev. 15).

Finally, seven bowls containing God's wrath will be poured out on the earth by seven angels.

1. *First bowl poured out* (Rev. 16:2)—This bowl brought sores on all who had the mark of the beast.
2. *Second bowl poured out* (Rev. 16:3)—This bowl turned the sea into blood and everything in the sea died.
3. *Third bowl poured out* (Rev. 16:4)—This bowl turned all the rivers and fountains into blood.
4. *Fourth bowl poured out* (Rev. 16:8)—This bowl caused the sun to scorch men with fire *(men still refused to repent and blasphemed the name of God)*.
5. *Fifth bowl poured out* (Rev. 16:10)—The throne of the beast and his kingdom became full of darkness and pain. They were biting their tongues because of the pain *(men still refused to repent and blasphemed God because of their pain and their sores)*.
6. *Sixth bowl poured out* (Rev. 16:12)—The river Euphrates is dried up in preparation for the *Battle of Armageddon.* Also the beast prepares for the battle, and demons are sent out who perform signs and gather their forces together for the great battle.
7. *Seventh bowl poured out* (Rev. 16:17)—Loud voices were heard from heaven, and the greatest earthquake men had

ever known took place. Every island will flee away, mountains will be destroyed, and great hail will fall on men. *(Still men refused to repent and continued to blaspheme God because of the great size of the hail).*

The following are some events recorded after the last bowl was poured out and before the Millennium reign begins:

I. *The Apostle John was shown a vision of the scarlet woman and the scarlet beast.* The angel explained to John what he was seeing. In the middle of the explanation, it was mentioned that *ten kings* would unite under the power of the beast, and they will make war with the Lamb of God and the faithful who are with Him, and they (the kings) will be defeated. The beast will come against this woman to fulfill the purpose of God (Rev. 17).

II. *The harlot Babylon the Great will be judged by God* and burned with fire. She had become the dwelling place of demons. She was the source of fornication and made many rich in her luxury. Babylon's destruction came in one hour (Rev. 18).

III. *The heavens rejoice over the fall of Babylon* (Rev. 19)

IV. *The marriage supper of the Lamb takes place* (Rev. 19:7)

V. *John is shown a vision of Christ on a white horse.* A sharp sword went out of his mouth to strike the nations and to rule them with a rod of iron. The words KING OF KINGS AND LORD OF LORDS were written on his robe and on his thigh (Rev. 19)

VI. *Christ on the white horse fought against the beast and the false prophets* and captured them and threw them alive into the lake that burns with fire and the rest of their army were killed with the sword of Christ. Birds were called on to feed on their flesh (Rev 19:11).

Millennium reign begins:

I. *The devil is bound for 1,000 years* by an angel with a great chain. He will be released after that 1,000 year is over for a short while (Rev. 20:1).

II. *John now saw all the saints sitting on thrones ruling,* and he saw all the martyrs who did not worship the beast or his image, refused to take on the mark of the beast were all living and reigning with Christ for 1,000 years (*First resurrection*). The second death will not affect these that have been in the first resurrection and they will be priests of God and of Christ and reign with him for 1,000 years. (Rev 20:4).

III. *After 1,000 years have ended,* the devil will be released and will gather his forces together to attack the camp of the saints. Fire will come down from heaven and devour his army. This time the devil will be thrown into the lake that burns with fire to join the beast and the Antichrist where they will remain and be tormented forever (Rev. 20:7).

IV. *The Great White Throne Judgement:* This is when the dead will rise, great and small, and stand before God and answer and be judged according to their works listed in the books. *The Book of Life will be opened, and anyone's name not found in the book of Life will be thrown into the lake of fire* (Rev. 20:11).

V. *John now beheld the New Jerusalem* coming down out of heaven to the earth. No more pain or sorrow or suffering for God' people. He who overcomes will inherit all things. God warns that all *cowards, unbelieving, abominable, murderers, sexually immoral, sorcerers, idolaters, and all liars* will have their part in the lake that burns with fire—*this is the second death* (Rev. 21).

VI. *Description of the New Jerusalem:* Lit up like a jasper stone clear as crystal. It has a high wall with twelve gates with names of the twelve tribes of the children of Israel (three gates on each side: North, South, East, and West). The walls had twelve foundations named after the twelve apostles. The wall measured 144 cubits and were made of jasper. The city was made of pure gold—clear as glass. All twelve foundations were covered with precious stones. The twelve gates were made of pearl. The streets were made of pure gold like transparent glass (Rev. 21).

VII. *There is no temple there for God is the temple.* There is no need for the sun or moon to shine for God's glory lights up the city. Nations of people who are saved will be there. Kings of the earth will bring their glory and honor into it. It will never be night there. The gates are opened all day. Kings of the earth will bring their glory and the honor of the nations will be able to enter the city. Nothing unclean may enter, and only those written in the Lamb's book of life will be admitted (Rev. 21:22).

VIII. *There is a river of life flowing in the middle of the city,* and on either side of the river was a tree of life that bore twelve fruits every month. Their leaves were to be used for the healing of the nations. There shall be no more curse. They will serve the Lamb, see His face, and His name will be on their forehead. They shall reign forever (Rev. 22).

Nugget: "And behold I am coming quickly, and My reward is with Me to give to everyone according to his work" (Rev 22:12)

About the Author

Linda Faye Anderson has served the Lord for most of her life. She accepted Christ at age fourteen. She was born the eighth child out of twelve to Pastor Reuben Ray Edwards and Florence Inez Edwards (Linda also has a half sister).

She has been married to her best friend and partner in life David Anderson for the past twenty-five years, and they are the blessed parents of two beautiful adult-aged children.

Linda has a bachelor's degree from Wayne State University (with a major in history and a minor in criminal justice). She also has a master's degree in theology from Destiny School of Ministry.

In approximately 2003, David and Linda became licensed ministers with Evangel Association of Churches and Ministries (headquarters in Roseville, Michigan). They continue to be members of the EACM under the leadership of Drs. Jerry and Sheryl Piscopo.

On March 15, 2006, David and Linda were ordained as Elders by Sr. Pastor (now Bishop) John Anderson at True Love Christian Ministries Church in Detroit, Michigan.

One of Linda's gifts is teaching, and she loves to teach and preach God's word. God has given her a mandate and anointed her to make the word of God understandable to even a child.

In December 2015, Linda retired as a Federal Officer after working at the agency for twenty-nine years.

Her main goal in this next chapter of her life is to be used by God in any way He chooses to usher in His Kingdom. Her greatest joy is experienced when she is doing God's work.

It is Linda's hope that this book will help new Christians on their spiritual journey. She has prayed that God will enlighten and bless everyone who reads this book.

To God be the glory! Amen!

CPSIA information can be obtained
at www.ICGtesting.com
Printed in the USA
BVHW072006190621
609773BV00001B/68